C

Love be with you always

Adulf

Love is
My Religion

Also by Adolfo Quezada

Compassionate Awareness
Radical Love
Sabbath Moments
Loving Yourself for God's Sake
Wholeness: The Legacy of Jesus
Walking with God
Goodbye, My Son, Hello
Rising from the Ashes
A Desert Place
Heart Peace
Of Mind and Spirit
Through the Darkness
The Teachings of Jesus
Transcending Illness
Old Soul, Young Spirit
A Grief Revisited
Praying to an Unknown God
Before the Night Comes

Love is
My Religion

Rooted in God

Adolfo Quezada

To Roy and Jill
My forever friends

Contents

How to Read this Book

This book of love is not meant to be read straight through; rather, it is to be read slowly, taking time to reflect on each entry. It is written in short, poignant, nonsequential paragraphs that offer a personal perspective about love that can be pondered and perhaps related to. The intent of this book is to invite you to consider how love impacts your own life.

I profess the religion of love.
Love is my religion and my faith.
Jelaluddin Rumi

Preface

Love is the force of God that creates heaven and earth.

Love is the breath of God that sustains my life. It is the spirit of God that animates my soul, and the lure of God that mystifies my mind and entices my heart. Love is God.

My love is rooted in the essence of God. I encounter that essence at the core of my soul in the quiet moments of the day. I encounter it in the bustle of the marketplace, in the solitude of the mountain top, and in the valley of daily living. There is nowhere that I do not encounter the ubiquitous essence of God.

Like everyone else, I hunger for love; it nourishes my soul. I am open to the love that is offered; it comes when I least expect it and it comes from the most unlikely places.

Even without an understanding of God, even without knowing the name of God, and even without the ability to explain God to my mind's satisfaction, I love God with all my heart and soul.

Love draws me to my Beloved, and my temptation is to stay and rest in the peace and comfort of prayer and meditation. Yet, love also sends me out to do its work. It is imperative that I take the time to commune with God, but it is equally imperative that I arise and go into the world to touch the hearts of others and to alleviate their suffering wherever and however I can.

Paradoxically, when I surrender to love I am set free to be the loving person I was meant to be. Surrendering to love frees me from the shackles of self-consciousness. It opens my heart to allow the outflow of love toward all beings. To surrender myself to love is to yield my most essential self to the greatest good.

I overcome the obstacles that stand in the way of love, but not by increasing my effort to love, and not by my willpower alone. Love comes when I prepare a place for it in the depth of my soul. It comes when I set aside my effort and my willpower and open my heart to the grace of God, who lives and loves through me.

The power of God is not in miracles that circumvent the laws of nature; nor is it to be found in faith that moves mountains or the will that overcomes obstacles. The power of God is love.

Because love is God, it is infinite and eternal. Because love is God, it is beyond my comprehension. Yet, nothing else is as integral to my being as love. Love is my religion.

God is love, and those who abide in love abide in God, and God abides in them.

1John 4:16

Rooted in God
Surrendered to Love

I wander into the desert and there, in that dry and desolate environment, I pray, surrendering my life to love. Even as I become aware of my emptiness, my heart is full of love for God and for all beings. What is prayer if not allowing myself to be absorbed in love?

If I seek love through ecstasy, I may find ecstasy, but not necessarily love. If I look for love at the peak of spirituality, I may find rapture, but not necessarily love. If I look for love among those whom I serve, I may find self-satisfaction, but not necessarily love. I don't need to seek love; it is always with me; I need only to *be* love.

Love brings me to my knees in humble prayer, and stills my being in quiet reverie. I look to God, not to solve my problems or to right the wrongs of the world, but to sustain me with a loving presence that gives me the strength and courage, wisdom and perseverance to face whatever comes my way.

In surrendered prayer I enter into the silence of my mind and the awakening of my heart. I do not abandon reason or logic; instead, I place them at the service of love. I do not fill myself with exuberant energy; instead, I empty myself that I may be filled with the splendor of love.

I do not leave my daily life in order to commune with God. On the contrary, life is where God is; life is where love is; life is where oneness is revealed.

How am I to love God? Is it with prayers of praise and adoration? Is it through religious rituals? Is it with tithes and promises of good behavior? Is it by building structures in God's honor? Is it through petitions for what I think should happen? No. I love God by loving every being whom I meet along the way. I love God by giving my full presence and attention, my kindness and respect to those in my midst. I love God by acknowledging all beings, and by honoring their individual uniqueness.

It is easy for me to become distracted from my life purpose, which is to love. The pace of life speeds up and vicissitudes occupy my time and attention. Obligations of family life, demands of work, and mental and physical exhaustion rob me of equanimity, compassion, and love. When this happens, I go away and rest a while. I allow myself to be still and silent. I sit with God and let myself be loved.

The purpose of my prayer and meditation is not to clear my mind of thoughts and fantasies, or to relieve the tension of the day. Rather, it is to commune with my Beloved.

Even as I pray, words get in the way, especially pious, religious language. Instead, I speak to God with my silence; I listen to God with my heart; I am present to God with my mind; and I yield to God my soul.

The essence of God is the ground of my being, and the star that guides my path. Yet, there are times when I am stripped of all relief, and left alone to find my way. God only knows the reason for this apparent abandonment. At times like these, it is my faith in God's eternal presence - in spite of my sense of abandonment - that sustains me.

I don't understand the nature of God, and yet I surrender to the mystery that draws me forth. What is this power that lures my soul? It is love, pure love, unconditional love.

I am not separate and apart from God; rather, I am in God; and I am the expression of God in the world. Love reminds me of that awesome responsibility.

Who is this God to whom I pray, that will not be boxed into theology or defined by dogma? Who is this God with whom I am so intimate, yet, whose mystery I cannot solve?

When I am living in the heart of God, my love is sometimes ardent and overpowering. Other times it is quiet and constant. But always it is real and life-giving.

The "will of God" means more than the preference held by a deity in the sky. It is more than the mandate of a supreme power. The will of God is simply love germinating deep in my soul, ready to be expressed into the world.

I do not work on earth for goodness sake, or to gain my personal salvation. I do not work even to seek God's favor. Rather, I work for the sake of love, without hope of compensation or expectation of reward.

As I enter my time of prayer and meditation, I surrender my goals and expectations. I surrender the myriad desires that preoccupy my mind, and the resentments that enslave my heart. In prayer and meditation I surrender my total being into the arms of love.

When I am depleted, defeated, and dry, I return to prayer and meditation where I rest, receive, and restore. Then once again, love flows through my heart and moves me to touch the hearts of others.

Conscious of God's presence within me and without, I stop and rest my soul a while. Daring to stay quiet and receptive, I am imbued with the spirit of love.

I am one with God, not because I deserve it or because I have earned it; rather, I am one with God because I am a human being. In life, in death, and beyond, I am held in the heart of God. My oneness with God is indivisible, indestructible, and interminable.

I am grounded in time and space. This is my human condition, my finite reality. Yet, it is this humble realization that enables me to ascend with wings of love to touch the Infinite.

What am I prepared to surrender? I surrender anything that inhibits the free flow of love in my life. I surrender my investment in earthly treasures. I surrender my collection of resentments that I hold against myself and others. I surrender my judgment of others, and my inordinate sensitivity about being mistreated. I surrender my preference of how things should be, and my anxiety about how the future may unfurl.

To surrender to love is to take on the attributes of love, which are: to be compassionate, understanding, inclusive, generous, creative, forgiving, accepting, and present.

My surrender to love may seem as if I am giving up control to an external power. But on the contrary, it is regaining control over my life by allowing myself to live according to my essential self, which is love.

Yielding to the will of love is not abdicating my personal responsibility; rather, it is acting in congruence with my essential being. It is not a sentimental gesture either, but a sober decision to choose the one thing necessary, which is love.

I surrender myself to love as an act of will. This is not a religious obligation or an intellectual exercise; rather, it is simply love returning to love; the part returning to the whole; the soul returning to its source.

I surrender to love, but I do so mindfully, willingly, and faithfully. My surrender to love is not submission, not vanquishment, not enslavement. Rather, it is my free will choosing - perhaps many times a day - to yield my soul to the force of love.

I do not surrender to anything or to anyone that is limited in any way. I surrender to love because it is boundless, free, unrestricted, infinite, and eternal. Love is worthy of my surrender.

The path of love traverses the land of pain and sorrow, loss and grief, discontent and disillusion. It passes through the storm of change and transformation, and ascends the mount of true surrender. I embark on this path at my own risk.

Love asks me to surrender that to which I cling tenaciously. I attach to love alone; but then, I surrender my attachment even to love.

In my surrender to love I no longer assume that I am the center of my own being; rather, I realize that my center, my core, my essence is love. In my surrender, I do not annihilate my personal self; I merely relegate it to its proper role as a servant of love.

To surrender to love I must first surrender to the present moment because that is where love is.

Love prompts my self-surrender, but it frames it with discernment, wisdom, responsibility and reliability.

There will come a time for me to surrender the life with which I have been graced. Death is the ultimate surrender, the final giving up, the last release. Yet, even as I surrender everything, I will realize that through love, I am one with everything.

Love is the essence of God
Ralph Waldo Emerson

Essence of Love

I dare to love, knowing that sometimes sorrow comes in the wake of love. And even in the midst of a broken world, I experience a kernel of love in every soul. Amidst hate, fear, conflict, and mistrust, I encounter the essence of love in the world.

Love is a paradox. It is the force that animates life and propels the universe, yet, it may also manifest as a small act of kindness by a stranger. Love is the primary mover of all existence, yet, it is also personal, intimate, and innermost. Love is the wisdom behind Creation, yet, it is also the gentle spirit that guides me and to which I surrender again and again.

Love touches my tongue and imbues it with words of comfort and hope. Love touches my eyes and awakens them to the splendor of Creation and the beauty of every creature. Love touches my ears and prompts them to listen for the music of laughter and the quiet weeping of a broken heart.

Love is much more than the condition of my heart. It is more than my feelings. It is the force that animates my soul and inspires my spirit. It is the impetus behind my sacrifice, commitment, and forgiveness.

Love melts me like butter when I experience the vulnerability and total dependence of a baby; and it turns me into hardened steel when I am called upon to protect that baby. My love responds to what life presents to it.

Love is not my action, although it can certainly culminate in an act. Neither is it a gesture that I make or a word that I utter. Love is the force that moves through me and affects how I live my life on a daily basis, especially as it impacts the life of others.

I come into existence with one purpose – to devote the totality of my life to love. Moment-by-moment I receive love; moment-by-moment I give love away. This is my daily practice.

Love compels me to live from my vulnerable self, my authentic self, my whole self. Love understands my self-consciousness and moves me gently toward self-forgetfulness.

Love is like an elusive butterfly that lights on my shoulder unexpectedly whenever it chooses. It will not be captured or forced to express itself. It cannot be manipulated or controlled, summoned or sent away. Love will not acquiesce to expectations or respond to demands. Love is free.

Love is surely in my heart, but it is in my mind as well. It thrives in an open heart and a present mind. But when I close off my heart or preoccupy my mind, my love has no way to be expressed.

Loving others can be risky business if I expect to be loved in return. But loving unconditionally has no risk because it is unilateral. Love is a gift, not a transaction. I give it without expectations, assumptions, or conditions.

Because I love, I am willing to be transformed for the sake of my beloved. Love is a catalyst for change; and it is love that gives me the courage to make the necessary change.

If I am not consciously present I cannot love because love lives in the reality of the present moment. I cannot love in the past or in the future. I can only love now.

Just as the leaves of a tree die and fall to the ground, I allow all that is false in me to also die and fall away. Then I witness the wonder of love that rises in its season.

Love moves me to sacrifice for others in major ways and minor. I never know what circumstances will arise. I know that there is no greater love than to give my life for the sake of another, yet, sometimes it seems the harder sacrifice for me is to give up my comfort for the sake of another.

I owe no one the gift of love. It is, after all, a gift. No one is guaranteed love; no one can earn it; it is given away without reason or purpose. That is the way of love.

Love is sometimes weak, vulnerable, and powerless; yet, it is the weakness, vulnerability, and powerlessness of love that makes it the most powerful force of all.

When I allow love to direct my life, I lose interest in what I crave. My need for control diminishes; my desire for power falls away; and I no longer seek to be known or understood.

Love is not virtuous; it warrants no compensation or special recognition. Love is its own reward. When I live in congruence with love, I am living from the nature of my soul.

Although love may stimulate powerful emotions within me, it sometimes comes without any emotions. When love prompts me to take action without emotions it does not mean that my action is loveless; it means that sometimes love prefers to do its work quietly, abstrusely, and anonymously.

Love can make me dreadfully sad. Because I love greatly, I am deeply anguished by the suffering that I witness among those whom I love. Love gives way to compassion and my heart is heavy for those who are ill or in pain. The death of those whom I have cherished leaves me broken and bereaved. It seems that suffering and love cannot be separated.

Although my emotions are real and are my way of expressing outwardly what I am experiencing inwardly; and although they may reflect the love that I feel in my heart; in and of themselves, my feelings are not love.

To love and be loved is to gain as well as to lose. To experience the love of another is to gain the gift of life. Conversely, to love another with all my heart is to lose my illusion of self-sufficiency, my tendency toward self-absorption, and my propensity toward self-indulgence.

What are the rules of love? What guidelines must I follow? There are no rules. Love is an instinct of my soul, an internal force that moves beyond external laws.

The inebriating ecstasy I feel with love is sobered by the pain and suffering that also come with love.

When I find myself at a crossroads of life; when I am perplexed about a decision I must make; or when I am torn between my conscience and my temptation; I do what comes of love.

Because love frees me from self-consciousness, I am not offended when someone mistreats me. Rather, love prompts my concern for the welfare of the person who mistreats me.

Love is universal and is not confined to philosophy or religion. Some of my friends have no religious affiliation whatsoever, yet they live their lives with wholehearted love, and affect others in profound and life-giving ways. These friends do not spend their time searching for the source of love; they just love.

If religious institutions or spiritual traditions had never existed, love would still abound in the world. After all, love is a fundamental part of life that transcends any humanly-constructed phenomenon in scope and comprehensibility.

Love inevitably manifests itself to me in the midst of my suffering. It does not take away my pain or minimize my anguish, but its presence is enough to sustain me through the darkest night.

My love respects the differences between people of all cultures, religions, and world views. It celebrates racial, national, and gender diversity; and it moves me to work for the well-being of all persons.

Even as I love, I fade away. Love diminishes my personal self to the point of extinction. The lover is absorbed into love. The part gives way to wholeness.

Love compels me to tend to myself as well as to others. In the name of love, I stop and step away from the heavy lifting. I withdraw to a place of rest and restoration, and take the time to look and listen. I remain still, if only for a while, and I rest my weary soul. I bask in the beauty that surrounds me and wants only to delight me; and I breathe the breath of God.

There are times when it seems as though my heart will burst with love for everyone. The more I love God, the more I love every soul that I encounter. But there are also times when I search for even a hint of love, but fail to find it. It is not that love has left me, for I know that it will never leave me. It is more likely that something is blocking the flow of love through me. Perhaps I need to unburden my heart with someone who cares for me. I may need to go away to a quiet place where I can gather the scattered forces of my soul. I may need to commune with nature and absorb its authenticity. One thing is certain: love *will* return to me again.

I look upon myself with the eyes of love. I behold the nature of my essential self and I see my darkness and my light. God accepts me as I am.

I want nothing more than to give up my life and to let love live in me and through me. I hold on to nothing, lest I mistakenly consider it more important than love.

Love does not force me. It waits for me to let go of all that stands in its way. Love stands by ready to enter my heart the moment I invite it in.

Love is the lens through which I see myself in others and others in me. I am different from all other beings, yet I am one with them as well.

Love is spiritual, yet it is intrinsic to all matter, all intelligence, and all life. Love is within me and without. It is the food that nourishes me, the beauty that inspires me, and the spirit that animates my soul.

The love I offer is unique because I am unique. We each bring love into the world in a way that no one else has ever done or ever will.

Love takes me out of myself and reveals to me the oneness of all that is. To love is to become one with those whom I love. I experience unity and commonality of purpose with them. Yet, in the light of love, I do not lose my individuality.

I watch myself for signs of lovelessness, including inordinate self-reliance, narrow-minded fanaticism, and unbridled ambition. And, although I allow my will to guide me, I make sure that it is love that guides my will. Ultimately, love is my North Star, my compass in life.

Love comes to me on a palette of many colors. I am overcome with awe as I behold the beauty of a desert sunset. If only for a moment, heavenly hues awaken my passion, evoke my gratitude, and bring forth my peace.

I do not dismiss duty as unimportant, but I do consider it of less importance than doing what comes of love. Mercy matters more than sacrifice; grace matters more than power; and love matters more than law.

Love dissolves duality and unites multiplicity, yet respects individuality. Love acknowledges commonality and similarity, yet recognizes uniqueness.

If I do not find love in the midst of worldliness, neither will I find it in otherworldliness.

I never mind my emotions, for they are fleeting; and I disregard my thoughts, for they are distracting. Instead, I am content to rest in the essence of love.

At the end of my life, when I am asked by death to release my hold on all that I've possessed and all that I have known; and when all that has mattered to me must be left behind; my love, which transcends time and space, will live on forever more.

The love of our neighbor in all its fullness simply means being able to say to him: What are you going through?
Simone Weil

Flower of Love

Love moves me to compassion for those who are suffering physically, emotionally, or spiritually; it prompts my concern for them and awakens my courage to act on their behalf.

The flower of love has soft, beautiful petals. Each petal unfolds a different gift: listening, attending, being present, supporting, encouraging, giving, nurturing, holding, teaching, healing, affirming, sharing, welcoming.

My love enables me to be with others in their suffering. I help carry their burdens, I mix my tears with theirs, and I dare to stay with them through their darkest night of grief.

Love does not distinguish between the lovable and the unlovable, the deserving and the undeserving, the acceptable and the unacceptable, the good and the bad. Love just loves.

Love takes me past the boundaries of my personal world. My concern for the welfare of others extends beyond those whom I know to those whom I will never know, yet, who are as important to me as those who live in my midst. Love is universal and boundless.

I must be a receptacle of love before I can be a conveyor of love. I receive love into my heart and allow it to direct my life. Through their experience with me, others will also come to know love. They in turn will touch the hearts of others. It is in this way that love begets love.

My compassion for those who are hurting physically, emotionally, and spiritually – especially those who are closest to me – is filled with love and good intentions; yet, sometimes there is little or nothing that I can do to alleviate their suffering. Love and compassion are sometimes powerless in the face of suffering. Even love has its limits. Even love must sometimes stand by helplessly. But my love can always offer my presence, be it physical, spiritual, or both. My loving presence is sometimes more important than anything else I can do.

Love has no prerequisites. I do not have to know others before I love them; I do not have to understand them, trust them, approve of them, or scrutinize them. Love just is.

Love drops the scales from my eyes and lets me see beyond borders, beyond differences, beyond fears and prejudices, to the union of all that is. I am one with everyone and everything.

I am interdependent with everyone else. At the level of the soul, love weaves me together with all humanity. The beloved and the lover are not in duality because, in essence, they are one.

Love offered is love delivered. Whether love is accepted or rejected, acknowledged or ignored, it is never wasted, never given in vain.

Love instills in me a spirit of forgiveness. It holds nothing against offenders, but it does hold them accountable for their wrongdoings. Love is not vengeful. Instead, it is prepared to absolve even the cruelest persons, and to help them change the direction of their lives.

Love wears many faces. It may manifest as a service I render, a sacrifice I make, a gift I present, a kind word I speak, an encouragement I offer, an affection I express, an offense I forgive, or a smile I give to a stranger.

My heart is nurtured by the loving gesture of a friend. She calls for no other reason than to see how I am doing. Her interest in my welfare is serious and sincere. I know I am remembered; I know I am loved.

Love does not lift me above and beyond my human condition; rather, it grounds me in a wounded world where I am needed to salve its wounds.

Love eventually leads to some form of sacrifice. I cannot love without giving myself away in some manner. Sacrifice essentially means giving up something that I cherish for an even greater good. It requires of me discernment, courage, and love.

Love is never measured or calculated. It offers itself lavishly because it knows no other way. Love empties out its purse; it brings down the moon and the stars; and it declares itself from the highest mountain. Love is not impulsive, but authentic and spontaneous. It is gracious in nature and life-giving in manner. Love's intention is always to seek the welfare of the beloved.

Love empowers me to serve others; it boosts my energy when it is low; and when someone's load is too heavy to carry alone, love gives me the strength to lend a hand.

Love is personal and individual. I may declare my love for my family and my friends, but the reality is that I love each member of my family and each of my friends personally and uniquely. Love is not for the masses or for humanity as a whole. It touches the heart of each person inimitably.

I am moved to forgive even the unforgivable; not because I am promised forgiveness in return, but because forgiveness comes of love, and love is my true being.

The greater my iniquity for which I have been forgiven, the greater the love I have received, and the greater the love my heart returns.

I love wholeheartedly. I love beyond sentimentality and the ethereality of moods and emotions. I love others without regard to their personal attributes or character.

I am willing to follow laws and regulations. That is, until they work against the welfare of others. I keep paramount the law of love.

I love others with power and intensity, yet my love may manifest in silent caring, small gestures of respect, and ordinary acts of kindness.

Love includes self-love, but not self-absorption. Love shifts my attention from myself to another. Even as I tend to my own welfare, my concern is also the welfare of the other. Love does not insist on self-annihilation, only on self-forgetfulness.

The love that emanates from the depths of my soul is the salve the world needs; but it is also meant for me. Love moves me to compassion for others, and also for myself. I partake of the gift of love even as I share it with others.

Love implores me to be gentle and kind with myself. It asks me to care for my welfare by what I do and what I desist from doing. Love needs me alive and well if I am to be one of its instruments in the world.

Love is not content to simply declare itself; it seeks to manifest in works and deeds. If my heart is full of love, my actions will reflect it.

Sometimes my love is silent and invisible. Only God can hear my pleas to a world gone mad. Only God can see the tears I shed for those who suffer beyond belief. Yet my prayers are not to God, but to those whose hatred kills and whose fear destroys. Sometimes my love seems like a single candle attempting to light the darkness of the night.

When I venture out into the world I meet strangers who love me even though they do not know me. These are persons whose heart is filled and overflowing with love, and who are eager to share it with whomever they encounter. Their love is contagious and it makes a difference in my life.

How precious is the love that I experience from those who call me husband, father, grandfather, brother, uncle, and father-in-law. It is a love that lets me know that I belong. It is a love with history, familiarity, and rootedness. It is a love that accepts me as I am, and will never be withdrawn.

What am I to do with a heart full of love? I am to share it with those who have not known love. I open the gates of the reservoir within me and flood the parched and desolate land before me, one being at a time. The love I have known is not for me alone, but for those who come into my life. For this purpose I was born: to love each and every soul I am blessed to encounter.

Love grows in the most inhospitable circumstances. In fact, that is where it gets its strength. Like the flower that sprouts through the hardened soil and reaches upward toward the sky, love will overcome resistance and be made stronger in the end.

Beloved of my soul, you are the essence of my existence, the purpose for my being. In full surrender I give up my life that you may live and love through me.

Adolfo Quezada, M.A., M.Ed., is a retired counselor and psychotherapist. Quezada, who is married and has four children and five grandchildren, lives in Tucson, Arizona

45906662R00085

Made in the USA
San Bernardino, CA
20 February 2017